"Jess and Rachel have taught me that being unshakeable means to know my purpose and moving towards it! Approaching life with fortitude and clarity and keeping on going is how to step into next level life."

LEXY LAND

CEO, Lift Bridge Bagels

"Next Level Life starts with being so clear and confident in who you are as a woman, as a person, as a being and being comfortable and courageous to step into that and live it every day."

HATTIE GREEN

CEO, Embrace Your Power

"Next Level Life is taking action, going for your dreams, going for your goals, not sitting and waiting. We are literally capable of everything and we have all proved that. At the beginning of our 12 week programme with Jess and Rachel, we had goals and dreams that we maybe thought we weren't capable of, that were out of our reach, but I see it from all of us every day, we are all a step further, I am so grateful and so proud of all of us!"

VICKY MORRIS

Owner, New Image Gym

"The connection that we have all made through working with Jess and Rachel is incredible. Being unshakeable to me is being unstoppable and knowing that anything is with in my reach! No dreams are too big at all and it's ok to be vulnerable because that's part of the journey of growing and evolving. It's being powerful and inspirational."

MELANIE LOVEGROVE

CEO, Lovegrove Wellness

"Next Level Life is having that faith and confidence in yourself that you can achieve anything and the confidence to share that faith with other people. It's also the knowing that it's all there and within your reach if you want to go for it! Working with Next Level Life has been a game changer for my life in every way, a game changer for my business and is having amazing impact on my family too!"

LUCY WATTY

CEO, LJ Your Virtual PA

"I've learned through Jess and Rachel that there is no dream thats too big, everything is achievable and you have a toolbox to do it!

CHANTAL DIMITRI

"Being unshakeable – its the energy! It's full embodiment of our discoveries, it's a woman who is whole and knows that they have a right to be here on this planet with a purpose and a mission and is willing to go all the way in any shadow, in any cave and face any fear to reach their potential and be that light for the world!"

TANIA KOULAKAN

CEO, Harmonize World

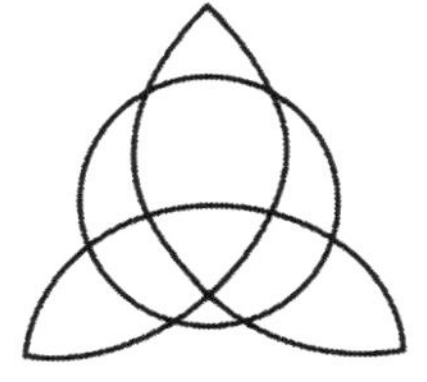

Your Next Level Life

THE BLUEPRINT

6 Steps to Elevated Success

Jessica Mclaren  Rachel Ross-Smith

Your Next Level Life – The Blueprint: 6 Steps to Elevated Success

Published by Next Level Life
24 Logan Terrace
Dundee
DD3 0ST
United Kingdom
www.nextlevellife.com
Contact publisher for bulk orders and permission requests.

Cover and interior book design & formatting by
Leesa Ellis of 3 ferns books → **www.3fernsbooks.com**

Printed in the United States of America.

ISBN: 978-1-5272-9417-2

Table of Contents

Our ask to you

is to be part of the percentage that makes this choice.

You all have the potential and ability and we have created this blueprint to aid you on your way.

Foreword

The idea came whilst sitting on the toilet. A lightning bolt struck, "You've got to put this online now!"

After pulling up her knickers and cleaning her hands, Rachel called Jess in a moment of excitement... their in person events were pivoting to an international audience. And in that conversation, Next Level Life was born.

Since May 2020, Jess and Rachel have created a global business which connects, elevates and empowers men and women to leap into elevated levels of success in life and business.

Prior to the pandemic, Jess was a full-time Principal Teacher in a High School and Rachel was working 1:1 with clients in London. Both are now fully committed to supporting 3.5 billion-plus people to leap to reach elevated levels of success, because no matter where you are... there is always another level!

Testimonial

I was looking for a community, I actually typed in Google search "a community for self-development" and I found you. I knew this was for me.

At the time I started working with you, I was in a job I hated, I was having panic attacks, anxiety attacks, I felt I was trying to juggle life, and it was entirely over whelming. I felt incredibly lonely, and I didn't know who I was anymore. I didn't feel comfortable speaking. So to go from that, to where I am now, I can confirm that I haven't had one anxiety attack!

Everything that was my reality then is far from the truth now.

I decided to leap into cyber security and working with you ladies I really expanded my vision and realised that I could move this into something more independent. I began to look at my core values and I realised freedom was one of them.

What I love about moving into my own space, I get to decide who I work with. With my own space in business, I realised I can impact others in a really ethical way and I discovered that for myself through working with you ladies. I have shifted into a place where I am vibrating on a whole new level, and I don't care if I don't know how to do something, I am going to find a way.

There is so much value in what you ladies are doing.

STACEY MURPHY
CEO, CyberStace

When you focus on the known,

you get the known.

When you learn to focus
on the unknown,
you create possibility.

What is Next Level Life?

Next Level life is comprised of three simple yet powerful principles:

Connect
Elevate
Empower

CONNECT is choosing to be surrounded by incredible people and relationships which are inspiring, uplifting, loving, motivating, and encourage you to step into your potential.

ELEVATE relates to every aspect of your being – and your commitment to evolving physically, mentally emotionally and spiritually as you create and manifest your next level of life.

EMPOWER is leaping into and living a life of abundance in every sense, full of fun and rich in experiences. Empower is creating an impact on the world around you and leaving legacy.

The Next Level Life Leap

is trading expectation for extraordinary.

It is building your world
through a high vibrational,
intentional action,
a leap out of the 'normal'
with such certainty that
the universe is shoogled
into following your lead and
creating new and previously
unimagined possibility.

Life, Death and Evolution

Waves rise and fall
The moon and the sun change position
Leaves on trees
Seasons

In every moment you are either on the living or dying curve of life, ascending or descending. In every moment, your energetic vibration is changing, and within every moment, you are always working with universal law – things never remain the same – you just have to look at nature to see this.

All that you have is right now and you get to choose what happens next – how do you continue to ascend despite the natural fluctuations of life? By becoming more conscious.

The living or dying curve is here for all of us. Society has conditioned us to conform to the belief that we have a finite lifespan, and that the traditional pathway should be followed. We are trained from a young age to go to school, go to university, get a job, work until we reach our later years, retire with a pension and then die.

What if you chose to be a part of the minority percentage of the population that diverts from the status quo and holds the riches? What if you chose to be part of the minority percentage that are really choosing to live? What if you chose to take the Next Level Leap in life, and to evolve at every step, every day?

Our mission at Next Level Life is to share this blueprint so that you reach elevated levels of success.

There will be adverse happenings in life, and whether its war or a pandemic, if a percentage of the population chooses to take the path less travelled and truly adopt an unshakable, unstoppable life and mindset, imagine the potential for all of us? We ask you to be part of the percentage that makes this choice. You all have the potential and ability and we have created this blueprint to aid you on your way.

Think about life – when you're creating, you are on a high vibration, you feel happier, things go well, people and opportunities come your way – e.g., school, job, marriage, kids.... Then what? You try to remain the same every day and challenges often appear because you became stuck and stopped creating. However, it's in your DNA to continue to evolve so you're pushed to take action. And when you ignore the signs, the universe takes over and you are encouraged often through unexpected challenges into another level. But by choosing and understanding how to leap into your next level, you get to create your life – you get to take control and you get to have fun with this!

Now that you have this book in your hands, the only thing between you and your next level of life is the decision to go for it!

The Quantum Field of Possibility

The Quantum field is where you let go of 3D reality. It's when you move beyond your physical body, beyond your senses, beyond space and time and enter a whole different reality, a whole different existence, one of pure consciousness and one of infinite possibility. The quantum field is your creation zone.

The quantum field is the invisible space all around you and beyond you – the space that fills the world, the universe, the galaxies and beyond.

The quantum field is a space filled only with energy – the energy of infinite possibility which you can use to create your pathway into next level life.

All you need to spark this inner alchemy and begin co-creating with the universe is awareness, clear intention (i.e., knowing your goals with certainty) and the willingness to let go of your current reality and leap into it!

You're reading this and wondering if you can – right? Wondering if you have what it takes to spark the magic? Well, let us bring the evidence. You've done it before, unconsciously. Therefore, you have this power, you just haven't identified it as such yet.

Think of a time when you were thinking about a particular person, maybe someone you hadn't seen for a while or had been meaning to reach out to. Your thoughts drift and you're in a space of nothing. Then suddenly you're jolted out of nothingness by the hum of your phone and low and behold that exact person you were thinking about is calling you! When you let go of the thought, the universe listened to your surrender and within the quantum space created the unexpected, so much so that right now you're acknowledging how many times you can recount things like this happening – a song on the radio, a feather falling in your path, universal nudges to remind you that you are fully supported.

Identify a time in your life that you have taken a step down a new path. How did the world show up for you? e.g., opportunities opening up, new clients, a new love.

See! You've just proven it to yourself! And now that you have the knowledge and the evidence, you can have fun with this and you can now consciously cocreate with the universe, in the quantum field in your day-to-day life.

When you focus on the known, you get the known. When we learn to focus on the unknown you create possibility, including accelerated results from unexpected places. This is the law within quantum science.

In the quantum field, scientists discovered that electrons move unpredictably and this is why possibility in this field is infinite. Anything can happen. It's up to you to use the energy to create it.

But how can you tap into something you can't see? How can you access this energy?

Humans have, on average, 6200 thoughts per day so it's not easy to access this realm. The minute a thought appears in your head, BOOM you're out of it and you've literally taken an electron and thought it into form. Now your thoughts are all things you have experienced, either from your past, or what you've imagined in your future. Everything you have imagined already exists but in the quantum field, there is an abundance of unknown, of possibility, of energy just waiting to be used to create what it is we want in a way you cannot even possibly imagine.

Now there's a lot more to it, when you enter the quantum, your brain slows down, much like when you get into flow state (transient hypofrontality). Not only does your brain slow down but your heart swells, becoming fuller, and together your brain and your heart create new frequencies, electromagnetic frequencies within your body. You create a coherence, a vibration that will act as a portal to your new future! A vibration that broadcasts to the universe that you are ready to receive!

Now that you understand the science, it's time to take the Next Level Life Leap.

The Next Level Life Leap

The Next Level Life Leap is trading expectation for extraordinary. It is building your world through a high vibrational, intentional action. It is a leap out of the 'normal' with such certainty that the universe is shoogled into following your lead and creating new and previously unimagined possibility. It's a co-creation with the universe that supersedes the expectational way of doing things and extraordinarily accelerates your progress.

Now get ready, because on this journey you're going to come across lots of different people who will cry Next Level Life what? Next Level Life why? Next Level Life how?

And why? Because for most people, stepping away from the norm, the hard work, the climbing the ladder of success is completely fantastical, mindboggling – crazy even!

You've got the 'norms':

- Kind, take action but are blissfully unaware as to the true potential available to them.

You've got the nonbelievers:

- Happy to go day-to-day, living for their next pay cheque, knowing that they've got their place in society.

The ones who love you as you are:

- They want to keep you safe; they love you and don't want risks to befall you.

And the list goes on. Get ready to spot them as we guide you on this journey of evolution.

So how do you take this leap into Next Level Life?

You are going to have to let go of old behaviours, even some of the ones that up until this point have served you.

How does that make you feel?

How many times in the self-development world have you heard people say – want it? Well, try harder, work for it more!

How many times have you yourself experienced burnout which often leads to blow out?

And then you need to start again and it's harder because you know the path; do this, then that, then.... You have tried and failed.

The good news is failure and the challenge it brings is a key part of your growth. It's led you to this point, to this book! And the even better news is and that when it comes to making a Next Level Life Leap, it isn't about hard work!

Let us repeat that – IT IS NOT ABOUT HARD WORK. It's about doing something different, unconventional and new! It's about creating a life you love that is fuelled by ease, grace and repetition of the new ideas we are about to teach you.

How To Use This Book

Create:

- Time and space to complete the exercises in this book.

Apply:

- In order to get results with this book you must commit to applying your learnings to your life.

Understand:

- That the Next Level Life Blueprint is something you will refer to daily until it becomes a part of your lifestyle.

The Next Level Life Blueprint has been created for continued success. There is always another level; you were born to evolve.

Step 1

Clarity and Certainty

Your mind's images are the blueprint to the world you are creating. Constantly changing your mind confuses you and the universe! Clarity, specificity, consciousness and decision are the starting points of any creation.

Thinking of each area of your life (e.g., business, finances, relationships, physical health, emotional being, spirituality), use this question for clarity on your truth and begin to step more into your potential.

If nothing was holding me back, I would...

Now you will connect to your why.

Because...

Using your answer, connect to your why again.

Why is this so significant? Why is this important for your life?

Once you have answered these questions, continue to ask yourself 'why?' Repeat this process 5 times, this process will reveal your truth.

1. Why is this so significant? Why is this important for your life?

2. Why is this so significant? Why is this important for your life?

3. Why is this so significant? Why is this important for your life?

4. Why is this so significant? Why is this important for your life?

5. Why is this so significant? Why is this important for your life?

To consistently operate on your highest frequencies,

it is important to understand the laws that govern our being,

the laws that govern our universe, and then the key is knowing how to be in harmony with the laws and be consistent in this.

Step 2

Acting As If Success Is Certain

You, yes you! You are consciousness looking back on itself. You are an extension of the universe. As you raise your consciousness you go beyond your current belief systems and begin to understand the next level of your potential. Right now, reading this book and choosing to apply your learnings is part of the process of creating new neural pathways and new belief systems.

Learning to utilize your belief systems in this life, by focussing on what you want and creating from that place with intention, is the way to manifest the life that you want to live. And there is no limit on what can be manifested in this high vibrational state of being.

Therefore, to consistently operate on your highest frequencies, it is important to understand the laws that govern our being, the laws that govern our universe, and then the key is knowing how to be in harmony with the laws and be consistent in this.

So, let's begin by talking about the Law of Vibration.

Many of you will know about the Law of Attraction. But the reason that so many people don't have success in manifesting what they want with only this knowledge is that they don't know about the Law of Vibration. The truth is, you can only manifest what matches your vibration. So, if you want to earn a million pounds but you constantly think like someone who has £1000, constantly worrying about paying the next bill, living paycheck to paycheck, then you'll only ever be delivered this value. You must be ready to receive what it is you want to manifest. How does the universe know you are ready to receive? Your vibration!

Remember we are dealing with the quantum field here. All of those atoms, dancing in the space around you and beyond, everything you both see and can't see is vibrating, including you!

What do you know about the Law of Vibration?

Viktor Frankl, the famous Austrian neurologist said:

> “In every situation, there is a space between the space and how you respond to it and in that space, you can decide how you're going to respond, now that space may only be a millisecond but in that space, you can decide are you going to react or are you going to respond.”

You are in control of how you feel.

If you ask a person how they feel what they're really telling you is their conscious awareness of the vibration they're in. If a person says, I don't feel very well, that person is probably in a very challenging or low vibe energy, and if a person says I feel wonderful, they're in a positively charged vibration.

So, understanding this universal law will support the results you get it in life.

Stop for a moment and think which vibration or vibrations you've been in over the last 24 hours. What impact has being in this vibration had on your experiences?

Everything you desire will manifest when you are in harmony with it.

The life you are living right now is exactly what you have manifested.

Napoleon Hill said:

> “Imagination is the most marvellous, miraculous, inconceivable powerful force the world has ever known.”

But you are ready to step into your Next Level Life and so, you are moving into new territory here. You are going through the gates of what is possible, but you can only continue past this point if you are willing to act as if success is certain

Note – We have said act. We know you are still getting ready to take the Next Level Life leap. If you're summoning up the courage, that's perfect, because step 2 of the Next Level Life Blueprint is acting as if success is certain. Why? This is part of the reconditioning process, because your brain doesn't know the difference between imagined and reality. Through acting 'as if', you are creating an energetic field with your thoughts, feelings and actions.

Are you ready? Are you ready to act as if your success is certain?

Are you ready to act with total faith, to proceed boldly onto a path which 95% of the population are yet to find?

Then let's return to your goals. You don't have to know how you're going to get there; you merely need to trust that you will and that you are fully supported on this journey. But you do need to know where you want to go.

If you worry about the how, you're going to start thinking of those steps again.

Instead, we are going to prepare you for the next stage of this journey, and that starts by stepping into your future self and imagining how the outcome of your next level life feels. It is when you do this that solutions start to appear, insights are delivered and the people, resources and opportunities present themselves!

1. Create your future identity board:

Answer the following questions:

Who is the owner of the life that you are creating?

How do you walk?

Talk?

Dress?

Think, feel, respond and act?

What does your perfect average day look like?

2. Create your future identity board

Find images, words and affirmations that represent your future identity. Collate them in physical form and create and display your vision board somewhere where you will see it every single day

3. Step into this identity today...

...right now, by embodying the characteristics of your future self as you create your Next Level Life. Commit to stepping into one each day until you're embodying them all.

Surrender is the practice

of allowing rather than opposing

the flow of life and learning to dance with it.

Step 3
Surrender

This is the chapter you will come back to time and time again. All you have is NOW. We are often asked "How do I surrender?" Surrender is being fully in the present moment, and being open to and accepting of, whatever may be unfolding at that time in life.

Surrender is the practice of allowing rather than opposing the flow of life and learning to dance with it.

Often it can seem an easier solution to resist moments in life, instead practice surrendering to and accepting what is. It doesn't mean you have to like it all, but it's the process of allowing. Through this life practice, you will see that you move into a space where you respond to life rather than react.

Through our life experiences, this has been one of the most valuable levels of awareness that we have come to understand, and we are excited to hear how it shapes your life.

Practice surrender, be open to the flow of life, release resistance using the AARR strategy (we teach you this in the next section) and watch as a state of ease and openness take over your mind and body.

Surrender is the ultimate freedom!

Know that life is happening for you and whatever comes your way is there to propel you towards your desires. Know that wherever you are right now is perfect. Know that wherever you are right now is both temporary and exactly where you are supposed to be.

You practice surrender using steps 4, 5 and 6 in the Next Level Life Blueprint.

If you do not
go within,
you go without.

STEP 4

The Unseen Forces

If you do not go within, you go without! As we have previously discussed, you are made of the same vibrating atoms that planets are made of, in fact the whole solar system. Begin to deepen your understanding, knowledge and connection to that which the eye cannot see and watch the magic of the universe unfold in new and miraculous ways.

The process of manifestation happens, through the thoughts, feelings and actions that you live.

Everything starts as a thought. This book began as thought, the device you use daily was once a thought. Your thought is powerful, and once it is connected with a feeling and emotion, the manifestation process begins. Look at your feelings as the gateway. Then, we take action. The action is the bridge between the invisible and the physical.

It's important to remember that what you experience in the invisible is as real as this book you hold in your hands. It is the process of manifestation that transmutes your vision into the physical.

This section of the blueprint is designed to help you to connect to your true power through tapping into the unseen forces and co-creating with the universe.

We have also included a resource kit below for you.

Meditation

- Sit somewhere comfortable.
- Close your eyes.
- Centre yourself through your breath (see breathwork).
- Imagine yourself in your favourite place in nature.
- Relax into this space.
- You may even want to listen to some relaxing music or even better, head to **https://www.youtube.com/watch?v=I61UvcT3HfM** to listen to a meditation we have recorded specially for you

Visualisation

As mentioned previously, the subconscious doesn't know the difference between what your eyes see in the physical realm or the invisible realm – your creation zone. There is great power in this, as you can train your subconscious into functioning with your future vision as the focus. This is done through the use of your imagination.

Visualisation allows you to connect with your dreams and desires at any moment in time, and the more you connect with them, the more you bring them into your life experience now.

You will find that with consistent application of visualisation you will begin to see your desires manifest quicker. This isn't something that is taught in schools very often, however it is one of the most powerful tools we have access to. There is no coincidence that people like Oprah Winfrey, Tony Robbins and Bob Proctor speak readily about this powerful technique.

The secret here is to be specific with what you visualise, have clarity and focus on the little details. It really is an incredible experience seeing your visualisation come to fruition!

During a trip to the USA, at a time travel was restricted, Rachel was feeling nervous about entering the USA, and so she spent a few minutes each night from 6 weeks prior to the trip, visualising the moment we walked through customs.

She visualised the customs gentleman like a father figure, who would joke and have fun with us, she imagined the joy that would be felt and the laughter. On arrival to the USA, the people in front of us, one an individual male traveler and the other an elderly couple, were both asked to access the interrogation rooms. The nerves were kicking in at this point. On stepping forward to the customs officer desk, he asked us if we were related, the answer being no, he turned Jess away and then, within a few seconds, changed his mind, saying "Do you live together?" Rachel responded, "At this moment we do." He accepted the answer and began to joke and have fun with us to the point that he grabbed his phone and began playing "Blondie." He called his friend over and spoke about us like we were his girls, joking with his friend that we were off to the beach! It was one of the most fun and easiest experiences of travel both of us have had.

This is just one story of many, where being specific using a visualisation technique has worked wonders in our lives and a crucial point in our life journey.

A really easy technique to use when visualising is, before you go to sleep, spend a few minutes visualising your desired result and stay consistent every night until the result has manifested.

Breathwork

A simple and effective technique that can be used at any time of the day, and before or during meditation and visualisation. this is an excellent daily practice to centre yourself.

- Breathe in deeply through the nose for the count of 3–5
- Practice filling up your lungs and breathing into your tummy
- Hold your breath for the count of 3–5
- Exhale fully for the count of 3–5

Prayer

Ask and it is received. The important part to understand here is, that in your asking it is also a key part to assume the feeling of your desire manifested.

Ask the universe every morning what you desire for that day, and as you declare, feel the feeling of your desire fulfilled, act as if.

To aid with your manifestation, you can ask specific questions. Ask for a sign to support your decision making or ask for something to be brought forward into your life.

Nature

Connecting with nature is such an important part of life. We are a part of nature and we evolve as nature does. Have you ever noticed that when you step out into nature your mind expands, and ideas flow more? You feel more relaxed and freer? So, with this knowledge, how can you connect more with nature, in order to connect more with the unseen forces?

When we do the things that scare us most,

we learn to replace fear with faith.

Step 5

Do The Thing That Scares You Most And Don't Look Back

Why? Because when we do the things that scare us most, we learn to replace fear with faith. Now doing the thing that scares you most, doesn't necessarily mean jumping out of an airplane or bungee jumping off the tallest building in the world. Often the thing that scares you most can be to feel your emotions, especially ones that you've tucked away or suppressed for a long time.

What you resist will persist, so be willing to AARR!!!

AARR is allowing, accepting, realising and reconditioning.

AARR is releasing the old and creating room for the new, for your Next Level Life.

Allow – allow the emotion to be heard and felt. Practice surrendering to the moment, no matter how difficult it may feel.

Accept it for what it is and understand it using the following questions.

How is it making you feel?

Do you feel this way in daily life?

When do you recall feeling this way and why?

Release – release through a ritual, a conversation that you have been meaning to have for so long.

Use one or more of the unseen forces or release through purging which can be laughing, crying, vomiting, trembling. Allow your body to direct you here and trust your intuition.

Recondition – affirm your new belief.

What are you letting go of and what's your new self-talk? Use affirmations, for example, "This is who I am, this is what I do". Move your body, be open with yourself and others.

A really important part of the reconditioning process is surrounding yourself with likeminded people who will support and encourage you on your journey, even when it feels scary, and you are stepping out of your comfort zone. One way to do this is to connect with a community or mastermind group, that's why we created the Next Level Life Community. You can access it here: **https://www.nextlevellife.co.uk/work-with-us/next-level-life-community-membership**

It is also important to create space. The new needs space to come in and you can do this using the Law of Vacuum. It is said that nature acts like a vacuum. To have the opportunity to attract what you do want, such as a better relationships, new opportunities and experiences, you must make room for your desires to manifest.

One of the fastest ways to manifest prosperity in your life is to create a vacuum by clearing space. This could be removing toxic people from your life, leaving the job you know doesn't fulfil you, creating space in your diary and letting go of habits and thought patterns that no longer serve you.

You are surrounded by abundance. Open your mind, and open your life to receive prosperity, and you will attract it.

So, with this understanding, it's easy to see why creating space is essential for your growth and development.

When you allow
celebration to ripple
through everything,
you share it with the world
and raise the vibration
of everyone you meet.

Step 6

Living Life Through Celebration

Living life through celebration is a lifestyle choice that connects, elevates and empowers humanity. Living through celebration raises your vibration and supports you to surrender.

Imagine lying on a beach...white sand... a gorgeous Adonis fanning you with a gigantic green palm leaf... your favourite music playing quietly in the background.

On the table to the left of you, a cocktail magically appears. It shimmers in the sunshine whilst its bubbles rise to the surface and magically pop in a beautiful lavender hue.

This cocktail's name is revealed....

Celebration

Wow! You sip it and feel it flow through every area of your body. You start to tingle, the corners of your mouth widen and with a heart full of warmth, of love and of gratitude, you smile more radiantly than ever before.

You ask the bartender, 'What are this incredible cocktail's ingredients?'... and he tells you – oxytocin, serotonin and dopamine

This cocktail is not just any cocktail; this cocktail is a magic cocktail for your brains!

So how do you release these chemicals and how do they actually help you step into Next Level Life?

Why is 'living life through celebration' one of Next Level Life's values?

You release these chemicals through creating opportunities for success, by surrounding yourself with likeminded people, by being consistent and disciplined in your actions and acknowledging yourself for doing so, by being an active community member, through showing up for yourself AND each other week upon week.

Celebration literally works wonders in the brain.

Celebrations actually boost your well-being, and this is true for celebrating major milestones and daily wins alike.

One of the main reasons celebrating is so important is because it reflects an overall attitude of gratitude and enjoying what you have in the present moment, instead of focusing on what you don't have or only on what we want in the future. And when you are in this state of gratitude you actually lower your cortisol levels meaning you are less prone to stress. This is yet another reason to take a stand and exemplify celebration as a way of life. When you allow celebration to ripple through everything, you share it with the world and raise the vibration of everyone you meet!

Our brains and our bodies function better when we give them both a chance to rest and recharge. Celebrating gives us that opportunity. Whether it's cake in the break room or a dedicated 10 minutes in a meeting, celebrating allows us to take our minds off the task at hand and focus on another important task on hand, recognition and appreciation for all that has been done.

How can you incorporate celebration into your daily routine?

You wouldn't forget personal celebrations, so why forget professional ones?

The Next Level Life Pledge

DREAMS BEGIN TO CRYSTALLIZE INTO REALITY WHEN THEY ARE PURSUED!

The world behaves differently when you begin to go after what you want. Wanting, longing, and wishing are not the same as pursuing a dream. They are essentially passive. Pursuit on the other hand, is active. Reaching for your dreams is thinking, feeling, and acting as though you know with certainty that they are done, and it shortens the distance between you and your desired objective.

I, ____

pledge to commit to creating clarity on my next level, acting as if success is certain and surrendering. I will connect with the unseen forces daily, I will do the thing that scares me, without looking back, and I will remember to celebrate every day. I will continue to apply this with every level of my evolution, with the understanding that there is always another level of me.

Signature: ______________________________________

Reflection

So, now you have the blueprint to your Next Level Life. Remember to use it every single day until you reach your goals. When you do, take a moment to celebrate your success – especially with us!

And then, pick it up and start the process again. You are a human designed to evolve, there is always a next level of you.

Testimonial

My gratitude goes beyond words on a page for Jess and Rachel, I feel honoured to be writing in their first book, knowing with absolute certainty the Next Level Life Blueprint is going to be a way of living for billions around the world.

I have had and continue to have 2–1 coaching with Jess and Rachel, and I am a member of the Next Level Life community.

Since learning and implementing the NLL Blueprint day to day I have seen huge positive shifts in my life, accelerated results in a short period of time, all while adopting a much freer way of living. Through understanding the power of clarity, surrender and stepping outside of my comfort zone daily, in the time I have been working with the NLL Blueprint, there are many things I have achieved, including setting up and growing a global business, releasing limiting beliefs, elevating each aspect of my life, and gaining incredible clarity on my next level identity and vision. Who I am authentically, how I show up as that person and how I celebrate myself every day are now some of the most important aspects of my being.

I am learning to carry my soul through life full of love and ease, with trust and faith everything is exactly as it should be. Thank you Jess and Rachel, Thank you Next Level Life.

With Love, Truth, and so much Gratitude.

HATTIE GREEN
CEO, Embrace Your Power

About the Authors

Before founding Next Level Life, we both struggled in life. We didn't believe that we could build a fulfilling life on our own terms and that life that was mapped out for us with no way out. BUT – we both had breakthroughs.

Jess

I was married, I had the perfect home, an amazing job as a teacher, paid holidays, a nice car, two kids... Everything society raises us to aim for, I had created.

But did I go to bed content?

No.

If I'm truly honest, as I lay down to sleep at night my mind went into overdrive. During daytime hours, I escaped behind the labels of mum, teacher, wife and put on a really good show by stepping into these roles. But when night drew in and the household fell silent, I lay next to a man, a great man, but one where the love had died. We didn't make an effort with each other anymore, and the thoughts that ran through my head, I still cringe saying out loud now.

"I'm being held back by my kids, if I didn't have kids I'd be..., when the kids grow up I will..."

But I accepted life for what it was. I had everything I was told would make me happy, things other people wanted. Who was I to want more? I felt greedy and selfish and so I compromised. I had settled. I felt guilty for wanting more.

With hindsight, it was no surprise that within a matter of years, my whole world came crashing down and I had become a divorced single parent. I had zero money in the bank and nobody was around to support me. I was presented with contrast and I was overcome with a complete lack of confidence. Nobody around me who understood what I was going through or how I felt and I had a fear of actually admitting out loud what I did feel. Added to that, I had no idea or strategy about how I was going to move forward with life and stay strong for my two young children.

Rachel

Roll back a few years, I spent most of my life not wanting to be here, and when I say here, I mean alive! I struggled with anxiety, depression and drug addiction for many years, I was constantly living in my past, not knowing a way out.

At the end of 2015, after another episode of my mental health having a detrimental effect on my life, I experienced my first breakthrough. I remember the exact moment it happened like it was yesterday. It felt like a switch had flicked on in my chest, and I knew from that moment that everything was about to change. The world around me was exactly the same, but a whole universe had shifted inside of me.

Shortly after, I embarked on a journey of self-love and personal mastery, and truly for the first time began to step into my potential and my truth. I travelled the world and stepped into the space of self-directed personal development, spirituality and business.

I am now more alive than I could ever even have imagined, and best of all I am teaching others how to transform their lives and share their message too. This is why we both embarked upon coaching journeys in our own rights.

We knew what it was like to accept life for what it was. We had everything we were told would make us happy, things other people wanted, who were we to want more? We felt greedy and selfish and so we compromised. We settled. We felt guilty for wanting more and we saw the physical and emotional impact of living that way. We knew we had to teach other people about the unlimited potential life has to offer, that there is a different way!

And so, when we were introduced by a mutual friend, we knew our missions were aligned and, within months, we partnered and created Next Level Life. We have combined our expertise, life experiences, and knowledge and have decided to share it all with the world, so that you too can step into your next level of life.

Made in the USA
Middletown, DE
01 August 2021